J. Postell

# That Ain't Love…
# The Home Girl's Guide to Knowing Her Worth

S.I.P. PUBLICATION

J. Postell

That Ain't Love

Copyright © 2017 J. Postell

All rights reserved. No part of this book may be reproduced in any form or by any means, electronic or mechanical, including photocopying, recording, or by any information storage and retrieval systems, without permission in writing from the author, except where permitted by law and for reviews.

This book is a work of fiction. Names, characters, places, and incidents either are products of the author's imagination or are used fictitiously. Any resemblance to actual persons, living or dead, events, or locales is entirely coincidental.

Cover Design: Matthew Postell

ISBN- 978-0-692-86164-6

Printed in the United States of America.

## DEDICATION

This book is dedicated to all the **Home Girls.**
It's time to take your rightful place.
It's time to take back your power.
Your WORTH depends on it!

That Ain't Love

## CONTENTS

**Woman to Woman**
The Home Girl………………………………………..11
She Get it From her Momma………………………21
They're Watching……………………………………27
Momma's Boy………………………………………...33

**Deal with You First**
Insecurity……………………………………………..43
Controlling……………………………………………49
Hiding Crazy…………………………………………55
Daddy Issues…………………………………………61
Daddy Issues PT2…………………………………...67
Sex Ain't Enough……………………………………75
You're Still a Gold Digger…………………………..81

**Wholeness Ahead**
Eyes Wide Shut………………………………………85
The Flash Forward………………………………….91
The Flash Forward Wasn't Enough………………..95
Loneliness………………………………………....103
Friend vs. Boo……………………………………...107
Setting Non-Negotiable Standards………………...111
You Have the Power……………………………....117
Worth It All……………………………………...123

That Ain't Love

Noun: *home-girl*
A loyal friend. When you need her she'll always be there. She loves you, corrects you and totally supports you. She's brutally honest and sometimes overly intrusive but most of all, she has your back!

## That Ain't Love

A man does not honor you by giving you a key to his house. A man does not honor you by making you his chick on the side. A man does not honor you by making you his "baby momma."

A man honors you by offering you his last name. A man honors you by making you his wife and in return, you honor him by accepting his proposal.

Refuse to be undersold, devalued and mistaken for a cheap knockoff. Shine on like the precious stone you are. Blind the world with the light of your reflection.

Know your worth!

J. Postell

# WOMAN TO WOMAN

*My femininity may differ from yours but I am all **WOMAN**! I embrace my sexuality and I openly celebrate being a strong, confident **WOMAN**!*

# THE HOME GIRL

*I remember being down south and smiling at every person I saw. I was always told that southerners are some of the friendliest people on the planet. I couldn't wait to be greeted with some of that good ole' southern hospitality. Imagine my shock to find out that people are people, no matter the location. I was especially appalled at the behavior of some of the women. When I smiled, most didn't smile back. I greeted them with a friendly "Hello" and very few responded. I would offer a compliment and in return I was given dry, "Thanks" or rude silence. Needless to say my friendly, outgoing disposition took a brief hiatus.*

---

How many times has another woman looked you up and down instead of smiling, rolled her eyes, instead of responding "Hello?" You may have experienced some women who have based your worth on what you look like, what your hair looks like, the kind of handbag you carry, the style of shoe you wear or *who*se name you wear. Have you ever pondered any of the following questions after an experience with another woman?

- *Why is being friendly so hard for some women?*
- *What is so hard about speaking to another woman?*
- *What can you really tell about me by looking at my shoes?*
- *Is my worth really attached to how much I pay for clothes?*
- *Can you tell a lot about my character from the name on my purse?*

I've been a woman for thirty-seven years and from my observation there are six types of women worth mentioning:

1. **Ms. Boogie**- *This* fancy chic looks down on anybody

who is different from her. She sees value in expensive cars, big houses and big bank accounts. She believes her success sets her apart and makes her better than most women. This snooty fox's cold demeanor isolates her from millions of great women, due to their minute differences. She only bonds with a select few and they're just as plastic as she is. She secretly wishes for genuine friendship but hanging with commoners would be uncivilized.

2. **Mother Earth**- This soulful chic feels sorry for people who aren't cosmically connected like her. She loves EVERYBODY but don't disturb her way of thinking, because then you're judging and those that "judge" get cut off! You no longer exist in her cosmic reality. Her response to questions regarding your friendship is, "I don't do people with negative **energy**."

3. **Hood Chick**- This chick is loud, proud and unapologetically hood. She tells it like it is no matter what. She's not ashamed of where she comes from, in fact she openly reps her hood! She's a bit abrasive but if you're ever in a brawl, this is the chick to call.

4. **Ms. Opportunist**- Guard any and everything near and dear to you. This chameleon-like chic, is loyal to herself only. She is in every relationship for something and it doesn't matter how long she has to wait. Although her motives are sometimes easily detected, be careful, this opportunist will pounce when least expected depending upon how bad she wants something. She will do any and everything needed to ensure a come up.

5. ***Ms. Bitter*** - Be careful. This bitter chic is armed with anger and she is not afraid to use it! Not only is she angry but she's also a know it all. She *"knew"* you shouldn't have done that. She *"knew"* you shouldn't have gone there. She *"knew"* you were going to say that. She *"knew"* you were here. She *"knew"* you were there. She knew, she knew, she knew. She knows everything except how to stop being bitter. How much do you want to bet she *"knew"* I was going to say that?

**AND THEN THERE WAS ONE...**

6. ***The Home Girl*** - This cool chic is a ball of fun! She is honest, loving, sincere and just the right amount of crazy. She's that friend that every woman should have. Everyone loves to see her come and hates to see her go. She's confident, smart and fun loving. She's not perfect however. Like other women she too has flaws. She's human in every since of the word. Her vulnerability, passion and love for genuine friendship, is what makes her, a home girl.

Do you identify with one or more of these characteristics in women? There should be a sisterhood among all women that produces safety, compassion and genuine friendship. Although I possess a little of each, my Home Girl side is most dominant. Every woman needs someone she can be authentic with - a genuine friend. Every woman needs a Home Girl to confide in, to cry and laugh with. I hope we all find and embrace our inner Home Girl.

## Answer the following questions

*1. What does being a WOMAN mean to you?*

_____
_____
_____

*2. How do you believe society views women?*

_____
_____
_____

*3. How do you view other WOMEN?*

_____
_____
_____

*4. Do you like women? Why or why not?*

_____
_____
_____

*5. Do you like being a woman? Why or why not?*

_____
_____
_____

*6. Do you trust women? Why or why not?*

_____
_____
_____

7. *Can YOU be trusted? Why or why not?*

_____
_____
_____

8. *Are women dependable? Why or why not?*

_____
_____
_____

9. *Are women naturally fake? Why or why not?*

_____
_____
_____

10. *Do you believe that women secretly compete with other women? Why or why not?*

_____
_____
_____

All of these questions are important. How you view other women affects how you interact with them and respond to them. If you view yourself as weak, a strong woman may be intimidating to you. If intimidation is a factor, you may not be as friendly as you would be in other circumstances. When you uncover your real issue with other women, you can understand how to make your future relationships better. Your approach and reaction to women and their behaviors will change if you are the positive change women need.

**Q: Do you feel safe around women?**

**A:** *No. I believe that women judge me strictly based on my outer appearance. The truth is, I've never felt safe around women. I believe that most women are shallow and insincere. The minute I turn my back, they will be the first to grab the butcher's knife.*

*Signed,*

*Annoyed Woman*

**Q: Do you trust women around your partner?**

**A:** *No! Women have shown me that they are not to be trusted around men - especially good men. The next chick could care less about my feelings. If she sees something she wants, she will go after it. To be honest, I wouldn't trust most of these chicks around my dog let alone my man!*

*Signed,*

*Untrusting Woman*

## How do we heal the years of hurt that have occurred between us?

My faith in women was quickly restored while watching an Olympic game. While racing, one female runner tripped and made one of her competitors fall with her. After getting up, the runner stopped and helped her competitor. Together, they raced arm in arm towards the finish line. My eyes welled with tears. My faith in sisterhood was suddenly restored. Women do love each other and it shows especially during the hard times.

Healing starts with you. If every woman makes a personal

vow to treat her fellow SISTER with sincere love and respect, then, we as women will regain our power. It's great to know your own worth but it is just as important to know and respect the worth of your sister. Make a vow to start over and try harder to be better at loving and respecting one another.

## YOU ARE YOUR SISTER'S KEEPER

RECITE THIS VOW…

***I am my sister's keeper.*** *I am responsible for how I treat her. I am responsible for what I say and do to her.*

***I am my sister's keeper.*** *I am sincere. I am trustworthy. I am dependable. My sister can count on me.*

***I am my sister's keeper.*** *My actions have an effect on the next woman. We will positively affect the next generation of women with our actions.*

***I am my sister's keeper.*** *I do not need to compete for a man's affections. If he sincerely wants me, he will make it known by his words and actions.*

***I am my sister's keeper.*** *My sister is not my enemy. I will not compete with her. We will lift each other up.*

***I am my sister's keeper!!!***

Write your own vow statement:

*Momma used to say,* **"Do as I say. Not as I do."**
*Unfortunately, I didn't listen.*

That Ain't Love

# SHE GET IT FROM HER MOMMA

*A teacher-friend of mine told me about a time when she had to write up one of her students for the provocative clothes she wore to school. My friend privately discussed with the young girl that the things she wore weren't appropriate. In the past the girl had complained about guys taking unwanted pictures of her butt. My friend explained that many of the problems she was experiencing with some of the males in the class could be a direct result of her appearance. The young lady had recently got into trouble for punching a guy in the face after he grabbed her butt in another class. Warning after warning, the young lady continued wearing what she wished.*

*The final warning came with a parent-teacher conference with the girl's mother. While at the conference the girl's mother said, "I don't see anything wrong with what my daughter wears. My daughter is attractive and is often picked on by insecure women, as am I. Long story short," she said. "Your issue with my daughter's beauty, sounds like a personal problem to me."*

---

<u>This Thing Ain't New!!!</u>

For years women have been devaluing themselves for "love." Some have ruined happy homes, lied, cheated and schemed in the name of love. We love, love. We are the best at romanticizing love but when our hearts are broken we are the worst at getting over it. When we experience a break-up we drive by the house, block telephone calls, fight, yell, cuss and pout. We vent, pray, repent, cry and cry some more. We make-up, get back together and break-up again, this time realizing we can do bad all by ourselves.

It has been happening for years – it just looks different with each woman. Some women are shy, others are bold and daring; no matter the woman, one thing is for certain, this thing ain't new and often times the cycle is generational.

The Cycle Continues…

I often wonder if low self-regard comes from a person's parents. Behaviors are often learned. If you watch your parents, friends, or family members misbehave, in turn, you too may project that behavior. You will either mimic the behavior you observed or pave a new road to life, health and worthy living.

My friend Elise's mother is, and has always been a trip. She enjoys the company of exotic men, strong wine, late nights and even later mornings. Elise and her mother have had several fights about her mother's life choices. Her carefree lifestyle and choice in men led to Elise's repeated molestation, physical abuse and a few other negative consequences. Up until a few years ago, Elise had also made a lot of bad relationship and life choices. She had been through several failed relationships, lost more jobs than I care to count and filed bankruptcy, twice. Elise had to make better choices or she would continue the vicious cycle her mother started.

The Road to Recovery

Slowly Elise started repairing the damage caused by the aftermath of her mother. She was in the process of healing, forgiving and healthier living. Today, Elise has a daughter of her own. She desires to leave her with memories of a happy, stable childhood. Elise's daughter is a wonderful child. Whenever complimented on her behavior and asked who taught her to have such good manners she replies, "Thank you. I get it from my mommy."

## The Blood Line Curse Is Broken

You don't have to be a product of your environment. You can create a new story with a great ending. You are your mother's daughter but you are not your mother. The truth of the matter is the only way you "get "IT" from your momma," is by accepting what she's giving. If you take the love from the journey and discard the mess, in turn you will WIN! In other words, some things passed to us from our parents are beneficial and needed. Other behaviors may be dysfunctional and must be discarded immediately so that it won't infect the next generation.

Are there some learned behaviors that you need to discard? Make a list of things you need to do in order to change some of the negative behaviors in your life and actively work towards changing the behavior. For example, I need to make healthier food choices. I don't want my daughter adopting my unhealthy eating habits. So, when making a list I would add eating healthier. Hopefully reading my list daily will help me began to reach my goals. Breaking generational curses will not happen overnight but with a lot of prayer and practice, eventually our lives will began to change for the better.

That Ain't Love

*Through a door, through a glass, through a screen, through the past, their eyes are* **watching.**

# THEY'RE WATCHING

*I recently saw a documentary about racism experienced by black musicians. The musicians spoke about how they bribed the disc jockeys with money, gifts and sexual favors in exchange for airtime on the radio. During the interview one man said, "We sent girls into the studio for the disc jockeys; this was to guarantee an artist's song was going to be played."*

*Excuse me?!*

*So, a woman would perform a sexual favor on a man she didn't know, in exchange for somebody else's dream coming true? Did she believe that being a groupie would somehow make her a part of music history? Did the artist that benefited from her generosity ever give her a personal shout-out for her contribution? Why did this woman put someone else's value higher than her own? Was this a learned behavior? By the end of the segment it was clear, the gentleman recalling the story was clearly, a pimp!*

---

The world glorifies twerking, fast money, body implants, and basketball wives. Popular social media sights display violent street fights, senseless murders and crazy stunts that could kill you. Unfortunately, the next generation has been left to fend for themselves. Half-naked girls are videotaped and applauded for popping their butts to the beat, while young men get thousands of followers by wearing wigs and mimicking women.

Television shows promote women with severe anger issues, prancing around with big fake butts, tarantula-like eyelashes, a pound and a half of makeup and a rich man to pay for it all. All the while, the next generation of women sits glued to the screen taking it all in.

The only positive thing some reality stars push is their new line of lipstick, hair weave or the new shoe line they have coming out. Where are all the doctors, lawyers, writers and teachers? Are their lives too stable to be deemed entertaining? Who will teach the next generation of ladies what a real woman is? Who will show them that good women are not a thing of the past, educated women are not rare, and wives are not what they see on a television show?

We must help our girls see beyond today so they can become the leaders of tomorrow. They can be whatever they want to be. They can do whatever they want to do. Nothing is impossible for them. If real women fail to stand up and set a standard of real living, then a lot our young ladies will have no choice but create their reality based off of the fake "reality," the media shows them on television.

## The NEVERs & the NOTs

Here are some things I teach my children:

1. Abuse should **NEVER** be acceptable
2. Abortion is **NOT** the answer
3. Love should **NEVER** be taken for granted
4. Teen pregnancy should **NOT** be the norm
5. Abuse of power should **NEVER** be excusable
6. Divorce should **NOT** be an option
7. Children should **NEVER** be misguided

The list above is just an example of some of the standards I've decided to set for my children. I want my children to be leaders. I want them to fight for social justice and stand up to hypocrisy. If I don't give them a standard who will? Whether you teach them or not, they're learning. Make sure you're their first teacher.

**What are your NEVERs and NOTs?**

_____

_____

_____

_____

_____

_____

_____

<u>When they watch you they're learning something.</u>

- *What are you teaching?*
- *What are they learning?*
- *What behaviors are they mimicking?*
- *Who will they become based off of what they've seen?*

If we refuse to teach values, model morals and show justice, how will the next generation be able to lead? Our children are watching. The day of *"Do as I say, not as I do,"* has left our children in a disarray. Mistakes will be made along the way. There is no perfect parent but with love, hard work and a lot of dedication, we can raise awesome children.

**GO LEAD!!!!**

*When I was a child, I talked like a child, I thought like a child, I reasoned like a child. When I became a* **MAN**, *I gave up childish ways.*

*I Corinthians 13:11*

That Ain't Love

## MOMMA'S BOY

*Natalie and Todd have been married for three years. They have a one-year-old son and a dog name Sadie. Todd loves his life with Natalie. He works like a man is supposed to do and he's there for his son, like a man should be. In his mind he's great. He also believes he's great because his mother calls every day to tell him so. Natalie also thinks Todd is great. He's especially great at playing video games, forgetting to pay bills and crying on queue every time she threatens to put him out.*

*Natalie can't take it anymore. She cooks, cleans and works hard every day. She often complains about Todd's childlike behavior. She complains about him not helping with the chores around the house. She complains about needing more help from Todd with their son. She complains about Todd forgetting to pay the bills. She complains about Todd being late for work twice a week. She complains and Todd "kind of listens."*

*In a last ditch effort to keep Natalie; Todd's mother convinced him to buy Natalie a new car, with her co-signing the loan of course. When Todd surprised Natalie with the car she was ecstatic! She never thought in a million years that Todd would "save" enough to buy them a new car. All was well, until eleven months later when the car that Todd "saved" for was repossessed, due to Todd forgetting to make the payments four months in a row. When Natalie complained her mother in law simply said, "My poor baby will never do enough to make you happy." Two months later, Natalie asked for a divorce. Todd agreed and moved in with his mother.*

---

Mothers are some of the greatest people on the face of the earth. Some of them make sacrifices for their children that can never be repaid. A mother prepares and trains her child for the world. She is the child's guide through the most important years of life. It is in this very process, that she will either help shape her son into a man or be the excuse he needs to stay a boy forever.

When a mother refuses to make, or allow her son to grow up, she is in turn his refusal to properly develop. She is an enabler who is stunting his growth and hurting his future spouse. A momma's boy may not grow physiologically due to his mother's coddling but he will grow physically and develop feelings for someone sexually and emotionally. He will one day enter in to a relationship that may eventually fail due to his unwillingness to be a man.

A momma's boy will be insulted when his girlfriend or wife tells him to grow up and be a man. In his eyes he is a man. His mother tells him he's a man, while still treating him as if he's her baby. He will view his sexual performance as man-like behavior. His age will tell him that he is in fact a man. When he looks in the mirror his reflection will be that of a man but everything else in his life will mirror a momma's boy.

The best gift a mother can give her son and his future spouse is, LETTING GO. No woman should have to raise her children and her man. It is unfair, unnatural and unattractive. A real man is not perfect but he is a hard worker, a provider and he leads his family. A great mother loves her son unconditionally and has a hands-off approach, while closely watching him grow into the man he's supposed to be.

Write a letter to your mother in law or your future mother in law. Tell her what kind of support, if any, you need from her to ensure a happy, *healthy* relationship between you, her and your husband.

That Ain't Love

## MEET CLAUDIA

**CLAUDIA** was a teenager when her parents divorced. Her parents were married for sixteen years. Her father was an addict for fourteen of them. For the life of her, Claudia couldn't understand why her mother waited until her father finally got clean to divorce him. Her mother couldn't explain it. All she knew was that she was done and Claudia was staying with her.

Claudia loved her father. She wanted nothing more than for her parents to work it out. She didn't care what people said about his past. She loved him, clean or otherwise. He was her father and nothing would ever change that, until the day she learned that he wasn't.

Claudia was twenty years old when her father told her on his deathbed that she was not his biological daughter. He told her that he loved her like she was and nothing could ever change that. After his death Claudia's mother told her the truth. She said that Claudia was the product of rape. Her mother told her that she loved her and how she was conceived didn't matter. It was the life that she lived that did.

Claudia hated herself and she especially hated the animal that raped her mother. She hated what he'd done to her. She hated her mother because she never told her; she hated her father because he did. Claudia felt worthless. She was the daughter of a rapist. She hated the very blood that ran through her veins.

Claudia's life took a downward spiral. She dropped out of college to pursue a career as a professional dancer. She never understood why she could dance so well. Her mother was an average dancer and her father had two left feet. *"The rapist must have been a good dancer,"* she thought to herself.

The interview was a success! Claudia was the newest dancer at Bottoms Up Dance Lounge. Night after night Claudia danced and men cheered. The money was great but deep down inside she hated how she earned it.

Every night she and a co-worker bet on which client was probably a rapist. Thoughts of how she was conceived haunted her day and night. She made random calls to her mother apologizing for being born. Claudia was done with life. She could no longer bear the thought of being the daughter of a serial rapist.

After three-failed suicide attempts Claudia was forced to get help - her worth was under attack. Claudia's worth was attached to who she believed she was prior to her father's bedside confession. She didn't know who she was. She didn't know whose she was. Where did she belong now? Everything she ever believed was a lie.

Claudia's road to recovery is going to be a long one. What will Claudia need to do in order to find the peace she desperately seeks?

What is your advice for Claudia?

_____
_____
_____
_____

_____
_____
_____
_____
_____
_____
_____

There will be women that enter our lives and we will be challenged to help them. You cannot help a broken woman gather the pieces of her life until you are whole.

*KNOWING YOUR WORTH HELPS OTHERS POSSESS THEIRS.*

That Ain't Love

# **DEAL WITH YOURSELF FIRST**

*Make Sure You're Healthy First*

***Insecurity*** *is like a fire. It ruins everything in its path.*

# INSECURITY

*I was following a young lady from my hometown on social media and eventually we became acquainted through a gathering place in our town. She was a bona-fide fashionista and her design choices solidified her gift for fashion. After getting to know her better, I learned that she was more than just fashion. She was intelligent and a master at business. If it weren't for the fact that she was so darn insecure, maybe she could keep a man!*

*After several candid conversations about her issues with men she eventually told me that every man she dated, left her. If she was not looking through his phone, she was looking through his drawers. If she was not doing midnight drive-bys to catch him cheating, she was accusing him of thinking about cheating.*

*Her excuse for being alone was, "All men are dogs." Thirty tissues and three hours later, I told the local fashionista that unfortunately she was the problem, not the men she dated. "If you refuse to deal with your insecurities, you'll continue living the life of a stylish dogcatcher."*

---

## INSECURITY

Everyone is insecure about something. Some people openly admit their insecurities and others mask their insecurity with emotions such as humor, arrogance, shyness, anger, manipulation and control. Whatever the method, insecurity needs to be dealt with head on in order to overcome it.

**Q: Are men the reason women battle insecurity?**

**A:** *No. Men are not the blame. It's not a man's job to do what our* parents should have done. I believe good self-esteem starts at home. Our parents are supposed to nurture and affirm us, thus giving us a strong sense of self. However, if you did not receive a strong sense of self from your parents it is now your responsibility to build it. Begin to gather the tools needed, to be a stronger, healthier you. I could blame my full-figure on my mother allowing me to eat sweets as a child. Instead, I choose to join a gym, eat more vegetables and make better meal choices so I may live a long and healthy life.

Before you can truly know your worth, you must get yourself together. Nobody wants to be in a relationship with an insecure woman. I often compare insecurity to body odor. There are two different types of "body odors" as it relates to insecurity:

**-The Dead Giveaway:** *This is the type of body odor that you smell right away. You can't hide this type of B.O. When you walk in a room, everyone is immediately alerted to your funky presence.*

**-The Hidden Funk:** *This type of body odor is not so easily detected. This type of funk is masked under expensive perfume and a "confident" smile but given the appropriate time and space all will know who the cute funky, chick really is.*

### Stinky, you aren't fooling us!

When you're not in a healthy state of mind, you aren't any good to anyone. You must:

A. **Love yourself:** *If you don't love yourself don't expect anyone else to love you. You must lead by example and show people how you will and won't be treated. People can tell if you don't value yourself. They will either abuse you, misuse you, devalue you or totally neglect you.*

B.  **Make loving you easy:** *Nobody wants to work hard at liking you, let alone loving you. Don't make it hard for others to care about you. Give good people a chance to show you how wonderful it feels to be cared about.*

C.  **Wash up:** *If you know that you suffer with insecurity (body odor) wash up. Don't get used to smelling bad (being insecure). A person can only mask funk with perfume for so long. Eventually the insecurity will come out. Get the help necessary to become a healthier (cleaner) you.*

D.  **Wait for it:** *That special person is coming. You deserve a healthy relationship. Don't give up. Continue getting yourself together so when he comes, you will be ready!*

That Ain't Love

*Knowing Your Worth,* **Does Not** *Give You the Right to* **Abuse** *Your Power!*

That Ain't Love

## CONTROLLING

*I overheard a lady discussing how one of her former coworkers was controlling and often belligerent. When confronted about her behavior, she often blamed others for giving her a reason to have an outburst. At the company Christmas party the woman's husband bullied her the entire night. With every drink the man grew angrier. After openly yelling profanity at his wife and threatening several workers, the couple was asked to leave. The lady said after seeing how controlling the woman's husband was at the party, she now understood the woman's behavior at work. "Poor girl," she said. "She's controlling at work because she has absolutely no control at home."*

---

One sign of insecurity in a person is their need to be in control. Trying to control a situation or a person is the direct result of fear. Maybe you're afraid that you'll lose something or someone, so you use control to feel more secure. No one wants to feel as if they are dating a parent. I have found that being open with your mate about feelings of inadequacy, help to uncover deep rooted, insecurity and fears, which ultimately strengthens the relationship.

### Let's Be Honest...

Opening up can be a big part of the fear that you have.
*How will he react when you open up?*
*Will you be rejected?*
*Will you be mocked?*
*Will you be looked at as weak?*
*Will opening up about your feelings make a difference?*

**-If you can't trust that your mate will respect your feelings, then why are you with them?**

*Reevaluate the relationship. Ask yourself if he can handle your heart with care. If he can't, make the necessary changes needed. Again, you deserve a happy, healthy relationship.*

**-If you can trust sharing your feelings with your mate but you refuse, you may need to seek professional help.**

*Maybe there's a deeper reason you can't share your real feelings. Did something happen to you that won't allow you to trust others? Get to the root of the problem before the problem, gets to the root of you.*

I too have had trouble freely sharing my feelings with others. I had to pray for wisdom. Wisdom helps in knowing when, where and whom to share your feelings with. **The day of people having to break through your "brick wall" to love you is over.** Controlling your mate will not protect you from heartbreak.

<u>*4 Reasons to STOP Being Controlling*</u>

1. **It's Annoying:** *Nobody likes being controlled. Especially not in a relationship. No mentally stable man desires to marry his mother. He may value some of the qualities his mother has and wouldn't mind some of those same qualities in his wife but he does NOT want to be in an intimate relationship with his mom.*

2. **You're pushing people away:** *If you don't get help for your controlling behavior, you will eventually push the person you love away. Visualize being alone in your latter years due to your own unhealthy behavior, should be enough to make you want to get the help needed to make you a better person.*

3. **It's Unhealthy:** Again, *get therapy! Sometimes there are deeper reasons why people try to control everything around them. Once you know what you're fighting and why you're fighting it, you will then learn how to defeat it. Find out what the real issue is before it's too late.*

4. **It's Stressful:** *Not only is your controlling behavior stressful on your mate but it's stressful on you too. STOP IT! The pressure to control the universe will eventually prove to be too much. A breakdown may be in your very near future.*

**Love is a risk and only risk-takers receive the reward of true love.**

That Ain't Love

*Better to dwell in a corner of a housetop, than in a house shared with a* **CONTENTIOUS** *Woman.*

*Proverbs 21:9*

That Ain't Love

## HIDING CRAZY

*I know a guy who seems to only date crazy women. It doesn't matter if he meets them at church, at work, or in a club. Somehow, they eventually turn crazy. The last girl he dated proposed to him at HER college graduation, after dating for only four months. The girl before that was great, until he busted her tip toeing around in his back yard at 3:00 in the morning. I asked him what he does to make women flip. He said, "They never start off crazy. At first they seem sure of themselves, sane even and then without warning, they transition."*

---

I know people that do a great job of hiding their "crazy." They lock it away and make the person they're dating believe they have found "the one." Every negative feeling and irrational emotion is tucked deep inside, until a situation happens and the insecurity suddenly pops! The first major explosion leaves the other person shocked, confused and depending upon how bad the blowup, afraid.

- *Why do some people seem to love chaos?*
- *What is it about drama that fuels them?*
- *Why does every relationship have to be chaotic?*

If you love to bicker, fuss and fight; ask yourself the questions below and try to answer them honestly.

*Do I love negativity? Why or Why not?*

_____

_____

*Do I desire a healthy relationship?*

_____
_____
_____

*Do I know how to have a healthy relationship?*

_____
_____
_____

*Do I know how to love?*

_____
_____
_____

*Do I believe that I am worthy of love? Why or Why not?*

_____
_____
_____

    Some people don't know how to have healthy relationships because they've never seen one. Regardless of what type of relationships you've seen or had, you can start anew. Starting new relationships with the same bad behaviors and expecting a different result is in fact crazy.

    Good relationships require maintenance, patience and a lot of dedication. Suppressing the crazy will get you into a relationship but like a volatile volcano, you will eventually erupt, leaving destruction in your path. You will continue to hear me say it, "Get help!" Find out what your triggers are.

What makes you revert back to those crazy like behaviors? Once you know what makes you tick, you can began the journey to healing.

## Are you ready to be healthy?

*In the left column below make a list of things you need to change in order to have a healthy relationship. On the right side write what you need to do in order to change that behavior.*

**Example:**
I have trust issues				Discuss concerns with partner

*A man can be your "BIG Daddy" but he can **NEVER** be your father! You should never make a man feel as if he has to compete with your past pains suffered at the hands of your father.*

# DADDY ISSUES

## PART 1

## DADDY ISSUES

*I always believed that I was different than other girls whose father had abandoned them. My mother was great and she made sure that my sister and I never wanted for anything. Not having my father in my life didn't affect me until I got married.*

*I married a great man who loves me unconditionally. He treats me wonderfully and the majority of the time I treat him wonderfully, but sometimes, without warning, smack dab in the middle of my marriage appears my daddy issues. When I pout, I want him to comfort me. When I'm angry, I want him to diffuse me. When I'm worried, I want him to reassure me. When I'm scared, I want him to protect me. He's my husband, not my father and not my God. My expectations of him were not fair.*

*There's More…*

*My daddy issues didn't stop there. I thought my husband should automatically know what I needed, when to hold me, when to touch me and when to kiss me. If he didn't do those things, I thought he didn't really love me. Without his knowledge, he was playing a game of chess and I dictated his every move.*

---

### <u>CASTING ALL DADS</u>

My father never stepped up to the plate but my husband did. Before long, I unknowingly cast him for the role of *DADDY*. I wanted him to be everything that my father refused to be. Expecting my husband to heal the wounds brought on by my father's absence was unfair. It was a role that he should have never been forced to play.

<u>Baby Momma Drama</u>

Your father's blood is pumping through your veins but his lack of integrity is not your burden to carry. You did not choose your father, your mother did. The disappointment was hers alone to bear. She was abandoned, not you. It is NOT your fault. Quit taking on the burden of others. Free yourself so that you can live a burden free life.

## **<u>TOO MANY DARN EMOTIONS!!!</u>**

I not only had unrealistic expectations for my husband but I also had too many darn emotions that were all over the place. Failing to deal with the issues from my past was driving me crazy…literally. I dealt with my issues by whining, pouting and yelling and when it all came to a head, I would cry it out in secret. My emotions were ruining, and ruling my life.

During one of my many vent sessions while sitting with three co-workers, a quick thought ran through my flustered mind. The thought was simple, "Be healed." It was true. I needed healing. I was venting to whoever would listen. I vented using humor and passion but mostly rage. My daddy issue came out in so many different ways. Sometimes I saw it in the way I parented, I saw it in my interaction with authority figures, especially men. I saw it in my views, thoughts and opinions. I could no longer mask the pain. I like so many other women needed help.

- *Do you believe that you suffer with daddy issues?*
- *Do you have unfair expectations of your mate?*
- *Do you expect your mate to make up for your deficiencies?*

- *Do you think your mate will hurt you the same way your father hurt you?*

Here are a few of my suggestions to help you:

1. **Seek good counsel:** *Get the help needed to move toward a healthier and productive YOU. Discuss why you may have unfair expectations of your mate. Discuss any daddy issues you may have.*

2. **Heal:** *Taking time to heal is a MUST. Healing is the next step in the journey to being whole. Give your heart the time and space needed to recover from the years of hurt endured. Once the healing process begins, every other area of your life will be positively impacted.*

3. **Forgive:** *Forgiving the people who hurt you is key! Forgiveness is not for others... it's for you. Making the decision to forgive is the only way to truly be healed.*

4. **LIVE:** *Moving on with your life is essential. After you have sought good counsel and forgiven other people go LIVE every day on purpose. Enjoy your burden free relationship. Make every day count. Being free of past hurts will revitalize you in every way imaginable. Enjoy the gift of LIFE!*

That Ain't Love

*A Good Man Is Hard to Find; especially when you were raised by a **GREAT FATHER**!*

That Ain't Love

## DADDY ISSUES

### PART 2

*Stephanie's father was a stellar dad and he was super fine! In school I envied the relationship she had with her father. I envied her mom too, but for totally different reasons. Anyway, Stephanie often complained about how bad her father embarrassed her dates. He'd physically threaten them, emotionally scar them and one he even "cleaned" his shotgun in front of, while giving a speech about gun rights in America. I loved it! He was the perfect blend of sweet and sour.*

*Years later when Stephanie left for college so did her virginity. She dated every bad guy she could get her little sheltered hands on. After her almost five-years of binging on nothing but bad boys, Stephanie was ready to settle down. She wanted nothing more than to meet a guy her father could call, "Son." She dated and dated and dated some more. She looked high and low but no one seemed good enough to introduce to daddy. Her standards were high and her fathers were even higher. Stephanie desperately wants to marry a man that loves her the way her father loves her mother. She wants a man that will love his children the way her father loves her.*

*As of this writing, Stephanie is still single but she has not given up on love. She says, "Prince Charming is out there somewhere and he will not give up until he finds me." I hope Stephanie is right because she's passed up a lot of great guys in hopes of meeting, the one she AND her father will love.*

---

There's something to be said about a man that makes a decision to raise his children no matter what. To be raised by such a man must be life altering. The insight a good father gives his daughter on life, love and everything in between is priceless. I'm sure every woman that was raised by a good father, dreams of marrying a man just as loyal, dedicated and honorable as her dear ole' dad. Unfortunately, most of the women I know that were raised by their fathers, are single.

I'm not sure what it is. Maybe a woman raised by her father, expects more from a man than a woman that was not. The women I know that have been raised by both parents speak very highly of their fathers but the men they date somehow never measure up. One woman told me that if she met a man that was even half the man her father was she'd marry him now. Another woman admitted she's single because she compares every man she dates to her dad.

Your daddy issues may differ from someone else's but they are still daddy issues. A woman raised by her father may suffer from daddy issues because the men she meets do not have the same attributes as her father. Her goal, like most women is to meet a good man, marry and raise children just as her parents did. The disappoint of her expectations not being met, time after time, eventually take a toll on her. She will either settle, thus never pleasing daddy with the choice she made or remain single.

Listen, you will never meet the perfect person. You will only meet the perfect person for you. Your parents found each other and made it work regardless of the opinion of others and you should do the same.

*What are your expectations of a mate?*

_____
_____
_____
_____
_____

*Will you date a man that doesn't value the same things your father does? Why or Why not?*

_____
_____
_____
_____
_____

*Is it important for your mate to have the same qualities your father has? Why or Why not?*

_____
_____
_____
_____
_____

That Ain't Love

## MEET NINA

**NINA** was diagnosed with Bipolar Disorder at the age of thirty-one. The effects of her condition had forced her to seek help. One night after she and her then boyfriend's bar room brawl, the police were called. Nina's boyfriend was hospitalized and Nina was arrested. She doesn't remember much about that night. She experienced what her therapist calls a "blackout." Nina recalls experiencing blackouts when she was younger. Something or someone would agitate her and suddenly, without warning, Nina would explode. When she'd "awaken" from her fit of rage, she'd either been injured or she'd injured someone.

For years she was labeled bad, a title that would follow her eventually into a jail cell. Once released Nina sought professional help. Dr. Reynolds diagnosed Nina with Bipolar Disorder and gave her medication to manage her moods. Although Nina didn't like the thought of being on medication, she knew it was necessary.

In an individual therapy session, Nina spoke to her therapist about her mother's fits of rage. She retold a memory of her mother threating her father's life with a knife on Nina's eleventh birthday. Nina begged and pleaded for her mother to calm down. Her mother left home for a few hours to clear her head. When she returned, Nina's father leaned down and kissed her on the cheek. He whispered, "Happy birthday baby" in her ear and left the house never to return.

Nina secretly hated her mother and blamed her for her father leaving. Like her mother, Nina knew how to clear a room. Man after man, friend after friend left Nina due to her violent episodes. She admits that each new relationship she jumped into helped to somehow numb the pain of the last.

Nina is finally on the road to recovery but the disdain she feels for her mother and the feelings of abandonment she has due to her father leaving, won't go away. She wants to be whole but letting go of old feelings may mean losing a piece of herself. Good or bad, her emotions toward her parents are the only thing that hasn't changed in her life. Who will she be without them?

What is your advice for Nina?

_____
_____
_____
_____
_____
_____
_____
_____

In life you will meet people that like who they are, good or bad. They will have every excuse to hang on to who, and what they are. Changing completely feels like betrayal to them. In these instances we must live a healthy lifestyle as an example to them. Healthy living isn't perfection; it's dedication to wholeness.

KNOWING YOUR WORTH HELPS OTHERS POSSESS THEIRS.

**SEX** *sells everything except wedding rings.*

*-J. Postell*

That Ain't Love

## SEX AIN'T ENOUGH

*Tiffani was celibate for more than two years. She was not willing to compromise her beliefs - until she met Shawn, an attractive businessman out of Dallas, TX. They met on one of Shawn's business trips to Chicago. The two had been casually seeing each other for a few months. Tiffani knew that Shawn was different than other men. She loved that he was focused and career-minded. Although she and Shawn's causal relationship was going well she couldn't help but think that sex would make them closer. She made the conscious decision to have sex with Shawn on his next trip to the Midwest. After several steamy weeks together, Tiffani was more than ready to take their relationship to the next level but Shawn was not. Although Shawn had strong feelings for Tiffani, he was not ready to commit to anyone.*

---

Many women often mistake a man's physical affection for love. When feelings aren't reciprocated often times the woman is the one left an emotional wreck. Giving sex in exchange for love will eventually leave you hurt and unfulfilled.

### Pull your panties up. He is NOT going to marry you!

One young lady told me she slept with the men she dated in hopes of the relationship becoming monogamous. It was if she thought she could somehow earn commitment in exchange for sex. The irony is that sex is often the reason "commitments," are broken.

I don't care how much of it you give up; sex will never equal love. Without love there is no commitment. It is important to **guard your heart and padlock your panties**, when in search of a quality mate. Trying to sex your way to a man's heart will only leave you with a wet tail and a broken heart. Everyone has sexual organs but good character is only found in few.

## You Attract What You Are…

I once saw a post on a popular social media page that read:

**Female:** I'm totally over meeting these "Do you want some company tonight" type of guys. Where are the real men?!

**Male:** (Response) There's a lot of confusion in what a woman wants from her conversation and what she wants from her actions. When you promote yourself as the party type chic, in turn you meet…players. Look inside for change and then maybe you'll meet a man of quality.

After scrolling through the page of the woman who posed the question, I began to understand the guy's response. The young lady had several pictures in seductive clothing. Her breasts greeted you before her smile and her butt was photographed just as much as her face. Unlike her pictures his response was appropriate and in good taste.

## It Takes One to Know One

If you want a good man, be a good woman. You attract what you are. Don't expect a man to take you on a date to the church picnic, after you just gave him an ear full, the night before about the many ways you can sexually please him. You teach people how to treat you. If you want a healthy relationship - be healthy.

Stop using sex as a negotiating tool to help improve your relationship status. Sex is great but that shouldn't be the best thing about you. You can't stay in the bed 24 hours a day. You must have something else that makes you valuable. Ask yourself, "What will I have to offer when I'm old and gray?"

What will people say about YOU? What else can someone say about you other than the following statements:
- You have a nice body
- You fine
- You're good in bed

There is nothing wrong with being attractive. I believe a woman should look her personal best but being attractive should not be your life's ambition.

BE COMMITTED...
- To loving yourself
- To your values
- To being loved for who you are, not what you can offer
- To waiting on real love
- To treating others like you want to be treated

CLOSE your legs you will CHANGE your LIFE!

**BE COMMITTED TO KNOWING YOUR WORTH!**

That Ain't Love

*More* **GOLD**…*More* **DIGGERS**

That Ain't Love

## YOU ARE STILL A GOLD DIGGER

*Lisa's only type was money. If a guy had money, he had Lisa. Lisa played hard and spent even harder. She needed a wealthy man that could supplement her lavished lifestyle. Her goals in life were to drive a Bentley Coop, live in a huge home and have more money than she knew what to do with. All were achieved but everything Lisa had come with a hefty price. A price that Lisa was growing tired of. Lisa turned forty on November 2$^{nd}$. The years of wear and tear didn't show on her body but her spirit was running on empty. She desperately wanted out but her greed held her in bondage. Without warning, Lisa's jail cell was flung open and she had no choice but to go. The man that filled Lisa's life with so many "good" things was ready to trade her in for a new, more improved model. Her replacement was an ambitious twenty six year old Dentist. Her practice was up and coming and so was the wedding date Lisa knew nothing about. The only parting gifts Lisa were given; were the shoes and clothes she'd attained throughout the relationship. The Bentley had been traded in for a Maybach and gifted to the Dentist.*

---

We know that toys won't fill the belly of a hungry child, neither will material things fill the void of an empty person. We must deal with the root of the problem. Most people I know who love money have experienced some form of poverty. The fear of being impoverished ignites the fuel of their ambition. Fear can't be the driving force and neither can money.

Ladies, people aren't giving up boatloads of cash for nothing. Something is expected in return. You must ask yourself is the trade worth it? Is the money and things worth your worth? Is there a monetary value for your value? Do we need money? Yes. Do we need self-worth? Hell yes!

    The next generation is looking to us for guidance A forty-year old video vixen should not be the matriarch of our generation. A Basket Ball Wife should not be what our young ladies aspire to be. We must constantly remind them that education, hard work and perseverance is the only sure way to respectable success. Wanting a man, because of what he can offer you is no different than a prostitute, offering sexual favors for monetary gain. Either way you slice it, it's "Hoe like" behavior. You're not an opportunist. You're a beautiful woman and you're worth more than you know. Be the value that you truly are and you will eventually attract what you truly deserve.

# **WHOLENESS AHEAD**

*Love is blind **BUT** you aren't!*

# EYES WIDE SHUT

How to Recognizing the Signs

*Guy had only been married a little over fifteen months before his wife filed for divorce. He admits to knowing deep down in his heart, that she wasn't the one. His first sign was when she joked about wanting to have an open marriage…in front of his parents. His second sign was when he had to talk her out of postponing their wedding - twice. The third and what should have been final sign, was when she did in-fact postpone the wedding. Unfortunately, his last and final sign was divorce papers, hand delivered on his thirtieth birthday. Surprise, surprise!*

---

## *RECOGNIZING THE SIGNS*

Many times you ask people if they saw any of the signs before the relationship went haywire and they say, "Yes." If we see the signs, even the subtle ones, then why do we continue the relationship? Here are some of the reasons I've been told people in relationships, similar to Guy's stay in them.

1. **Loneliness:** *Some feel that a companion, even an incompatible one, is still better than no companion at all. Thus settling for "love." They fear loneliness more than incompatibility.*

2. **Insecure:** *Insecurity is one of the main reasons people ignore unhealthy dating signs. They're simply happy to have someone. They settle for less because they believe that no one else will want them.*

3. **Condemnation:** *Believe it or not some people believe that a dysfunctional relationship is all they deserve. They're not afraid of being alone nor are they insecure. Maybe they hurt a past lover or*

were the cause of a relationship ending. Whatever the reason, they believe that their past behavior, warrants their present misery.

4. **Good as it Gets:** *Many settle because the standards they once set now seem unrealistic. When love leads to disappointment after disappointment, settling seems like a decent choice. They fool themselves into thinking that they should be grateful that they found a "half decent" human being in this world. They believe this is as good as it gets.*

I believe that everybody plays the fool. This simply means that everyone, at least once, has either been involved in or will be in an unhealthy relationship. However, making sure that you don't continue to be the one "playing the fool" is what really matters. Learning from your past mistakes is a must if you want to enjoy a healthy existence.

Guy and his girlfriend have had an on again, off again relationship for two years. He ignored the signs that told him to break it off due to his emotions. Emotions will cloud your judgment every time. You must detach from your feelings when trying to make a clean break from an unhealthy relationship.

## Guy's Signs:

1. **The "Whatever you Like" (Similar Interests):** Guy said that he and his ex-bonded extremely fast because they liked so many of the same things. Whatever he liked, she liked. Whatever he enjoyed, she enjoyed. What he later learned was that most of the things she said interested her, were not interesting once they became exclusive.

*If it looks like a duck and quacks like a duck…it might just be a chicken, mimicking a duck. If something inside of you says, "something isn't right" believe it. If it's too good to be true, it probably is. Only time will tell so WAIT ON TIME!*

2. **Quick Promotion:** Guy's ex wanted their relationship to move very quickly. She sought quick promotion with limited trust. The goal was clear. She would soon sheepishly, demand a title, to secure her position.

*You can't rush love. Take the time needed to get to know the other person. YOU CAN ONLY HIDE CRAZY FOR SO LONG. Over time, the real intent of a person will be revealed. Wait until you're ready. If the person is for you, they will wait.*

3. **Clinginess:** Guy often felt smothered in his relationship. In the beginning he thought it was cute. "She needed me and I loved being needed." Soon her cute, "Baby I need you" rants, became overwhelming and unbearable.

*It's a great feeling to know that the one you love does love you back but it becomes unhealthy when the person you are dating becomes possessive. Possessive and aggressive behavior is a form of abuse.*

4. **The Fits of rage:** Guy watched his once cool, calm girlfriend grow increasingly angry as their relationship progressed. She didn't like his female friends, nor did she want him talking to them. She began to express anger by verbally abusing him. The verbal abuse became increasingly violent and often led to physical confrontations.

*Anger is a natural emotion. We all feel angry from time to time. When expressed negatively, however, anger becomes dangerous and unhealthy. When you realize that you are dating someone who is abusive, you need to get out of the relationship immediately. Real love doesn't involve pain.*

5. **The Sex It Away:** Guy admitted that a lot of the problems with his ex were overlooked due to good sex. He desperately wanted to end the relationship but his physical and emotional desires made it virtually impossible. His brain told him to run but his heart held the possibility of escape hostage.

*SEX IS NOT A SUBSTITUTE FOR A GOOD RELATIONSHIP! Once sex is introduced in a relationship your emotions cannot be trusted. There must be a solid foundation and a healthy relationship to build upon.*

*If you could see the* **future**, *would you* **change** *your now?*

That Ain't Love

# THE FLASH FORWARD

### Imagine the Outcome to Avoid Living the Mistake

*I remember dating a guy that didn't require a "Flash Forward" I knew exactly who he was and what he had to offer. He was a bad boy and I liked it. I also liked his milk chocolate skin, his big broad shoulders, his cunning bright smile and his full of life personality. He was the devil and I knew it. When the relationship was over, I was left with a bad reputation, very little credibility and enough drama to fill the pages of two novels. I touched the fire and it had burned my character.*

---

The best part of a nightmare is waking up and realizing it was just a dream. The flash forward is just that. It's imagining a realistic outcome of the situation that can help avoid tragedy. I often tell people to take the signs that they often ignore about someone and create a flash-forward of what a relationship with that person would look like. If they're moody, don't ignore it and assume they'll change. Do a "flash forward" of how it would be dating a moody person. Imagine having to walk around worried about how this person will change from day to day. Is this someone you'd enjoy spending your life with? If not get out of the relationship before it's too late.

*Listed below is a small example of character traits. Circle the positive character traits and put a ---- through the negative character traits.*

---

| -Friendly | -Confident | -Ambitious |
| -Honest | -Protective | -Shy |

| | | |
|---|---|---|
| -Talkative | -Rowdy | -Sly |
| -Annoying | -Angry | -Proud |
| -Bossy | -Determined | -Sincere |
| -Lazy | -Jealous | -Disciplined |
| -Thoughtful | -Gullible | -Conceited |
| -Peaceful | -Quiet | -Impulsive |

When looking at a list of character traits, it is easy to point out the good traits versus the negative ones. It gets a little more difficult when you think about the person you're dating. You overlook the sly, jealous guy because he is determined, sexy and ambitious. You overlook jealousy, in fact some women think it's cute until he turns abusive. You hate their ways but it's too late because you think you are in love.

Make your own list. Put the person's name you're either dating or wanting to date at the top of the list. List all of their known character traits. Put a circle around the positive traits and a ------ through the negative traits. Then go back and put a square around all the negative traits that you have ignored. Once you're done ask yourself if you've compromised your standards in any way.

It's very hard to argue with paper. The list is a visual aid to help you either change your negative behavior or to help you continue making healthy relationship choices. Remember that a "flash forward" is the outcome reached, based upon your imagination of the future. The purpose of the exercise is to help you imagine the outcome so that you will avoid living the mistake.

*Being warned that the fire was **HOT** wasn't enough for you. You **HAD** to touch it!*

That Ain't Love

## The Flash Forward Wasn't Enough

So you took the mental snapshot but it wasn't enough to make you reconsider. Whether the breakup was mutual, heartbreaking or a scene straight out of the movie, "War of the Roses," the good news is you survived. But did you **RECOVER**? Often times you leave a bad situation, so happy to have survived that you forget about the recovery process.

If you've ever been in the hospital or known someone who has, you know how great it feels to be **DISCHARGED**. During the discharge process, the nurse comes in and explains your **AFTERCARE** plan to ensure a full recovery. Once home, you look over the paperwork recovery instructions and read any important details you may have missed. Sometime later, you recover. If only breakups were that easy. Imagine a packet of information, full of AFTERCARE answers, to some of those questions that arise after a breakup. Answers to questions like:

1. *How long will it take to recover?*
2. *How do I prevent going through this again?*
3. *Why didn't I see this coming?*

If there were a packet that prepared your heart for the aftermath of a breakup would you follow it? Would you take the necessary steps to fully recover? Surviving a bad relationship or situation is only part of the process. Recovery from what has been done, seen, or said is needed in order to move forward.

Jumping straight into another relationship after a breakup is an example of surviving but not recovering. It is also unfair to your current dating partner. Anything done in your current relationship that reminds you of your past hurts will destroy any possibility of a healthy start. In order to properly heal, you must commit to taking the necessary time needed.

## **_COMMIT TO THE VICTORY_**

If you were in an unhealthy relationship and managed to escape…commit to the victory. Going back to a bad relationship should **_NEVER_** be an option. Stay committed to a full recovery, so that you will be completely ready when the time comes to date again. A FULL RECOVERY also benefits your new partner. The less mess they have to deal with from your previous relationship, the better.

## MEET PATRICE

**PATRICE** has been married for nine years. She and her husband have three handsome sons. Patrice's husband loves his wife and provides greatly for their children. Their eldest son is his father through and through. Their middle son is the perfect combination of Patrice and her husband. The baby boy however, may or may not belong to Patrice's husband. If Patrice had to admit who her son resembled most, it would be Quincy. Quincy was Patrice's first love and since the birth of her son, her arch nemesis.

Patrice doesn't want anything to do with Quincy, nor the huge mistake she made with him two years and nine months ago. She'd love to prove to him that her son is not his but it would take a biological miracle for that to happen. Patrice and her husband were going through a really rough time when the affair happened. They only communicated when necessary and their sex life was nonexistent. Her husband's sleeping quarters were in the family room, complete with the queen size blowup mattress they purchased when they were first married.

Neither understood what was happening to the marriage. They were growing apart and didn't know how to stop it. After speaking to a friend about the situation the two agreed to marital counseling. After a few sessions Patrice decided to end her affair with Quincy and work on her marriage. Patrice prayed that the new life growing inside of her belonged to her husband. Dreams of her baby boy having Quincy's face and her husband's name gave her nightmares.

Quincy begged for Patrice to get a DNA test but she

refused. She wanted nothing more than to get a DNA test but she feared the worst. She wanted to tell her husband all about the affair but she feared what he might do. Would he understand the mistake she'd made? Would he forgive her? Patrice was overwhelmed with guilt. She didn't want Quincy to tell her husband before she could.

Patrice was ready to let out her secret. She decided to tell her husband everything. She was going to tell him that when she met Quincy, she was lonely. The two of them weren't talking and Quincy loved listening to her. Despite the affair her husband was the only man she ever loved. She wanted him and him alone.

Patrice was finally ready to tell her husband everything. She was willing to do whatever it took to move forward. She walked in the house and there, with her husband, sat Quincy.

What if any advice would you give Patrice and her husband?

_____
_____
_____
_____
_____
_____
_____
_____
_____
_____
_____

When you don't know what to do for a fellow sister in need, just being there for her is key. Sometimes having a shoulder to cry on is far better than words at that moment. Before speaking, pray about what to say and how to say it. Kind words during a difficult time shine like a bright light in the midst of darkness.

*KNOWING YOUR WORTH HELPS OTHERS POSSESS THEIRS.*

That Ain't Love

*If **loneliness** were a snake, it would have* **STRANGLED** *you to death.*

That Ain't Love

## LONELINESS

### The Journey to Enjoying Me

*My cousin's friend recently went through a very bad divorce. He and his ex-wife were fighting over everything, including the dog. From a distance I watched their once true love, turn into pure disgust. I watched her waste no time introducing her new boo to all of social media. My cousin's friend refused to let time heal his wounds. Before long, he was engaged to a dead ringer for his ex-wife. When I asked my cousin why his friend rushed into yet another relationship he said, "A man comes in this world alone and he'll leave it alone. No since in him sleeping alone too."*

---

I know a lot of people that are afraid of being alone. They treat loneliness as if it is a plague. They're afraid of being alone so they run from relationship to relationship, desperately trying to avoid being by themselves. These people commit to relationships full of heartache just for the sake of having someone. When faced with the decision of choosing between an unhealthy partner and loneliness, they often choose an unhealthy partner.

Some people ONLY feel valued or valuable, once in a relationship. Validation should not be based on who you are or aren't dating. My advice is to first learn how to enjoy you. Learn how to laugh at your own jokes. Treat yourself to a night out. Compliment yourself. LOVE YOU! Don't wait for someone else to do it. Asking someone to love you without first loving yourself, is an unfair burden for them to have to carry. When depending on others love to fulfill you, you become more susceptible to abuse and ultimately unfulfillment.

**ACTIVITY:**

Make a list of things that you enjoy doing. Then don't ask anyone to do them with you. Just enjoy…YOU!

_____

_____

_____

_____

_____

_____

_____

**Outing Ideas:**

- Movies
- Spa
- Biking
- Dinner
- A game
- Shopping
- Park
- Dancing
- Church
- Skating
- Vacation
- Hiking

*A true* **FRIEND** *is the best* ***possession.***
       *-Anonymous*

That Ain't Love

## FRIEND VS. BOO

*Najee and his best friend Tamela have been hanging since second grade. They were together so much, that they were often mistaken for brother and sister. Najee loved Tamela like he'd never loved another woman. They were friends and that trumped any romantic relationship he'd ever had. When Tamela's ex-boyfriend Murphy broke her heart, Najee was there with a box of tissues for her and a beat down for him.*

*One night, Najee dreamed that Tamela married his brother Nate and he woke up furious! He called Nate and demanded to know what was going on between him and Tamela. Nate swore that he and Tamela were just friends. Once diffused, Nate gave Najee advice that would forever change his and Tamela's life. He said, "Najee. If you don't tell Tamela how much you love her…somebody else will." Two days later Najee did just that. Today, Najee and Tamela are happily married with twin girls and a dog named, Murphy.*

---

Many times a potentially good relationship is ruined because a solid friendship was never established. Taking time to truly get to know someone is imperative. The more time you spend with a person, the more you learn about them.

In a platonic relationship you never hear about someone introducing a new friend to other people as their "best friend," especially after knowing them for a month. If you wouldn't rush making someone your best friend, then why would you do it in your dating relationships?

I often suggest that when dating that you **W**atch- **W**ait- **L**isten and then **L**ove (W.W.L.L.)

- **Watch**ing the actions and behaviors of a potential partner helps to make an informed decision about whether or not to continue dating them. Sometimes, we fail to see the signs that are right in front of us because we are either rushing the relationship or choosing to ignore them due to feelings for the other person. Ignoring the signs that a relationship won't work will only lead to heartbreak.
- **Wait**ing to make a decision like dating someone exclusively is very important. Waiting gives you a chance to see the character of a person. What makes them happy? What makes them sad? What makes them jealous or angry? Taking the time necessary to get to know your partner will help determine if this is truly the person for you to marry.
- **Listen**ing to your potential partner helps you make informed decisions about them and the relationship. Sooner or later what is truly in their heart; will come out of their mouth.
- **Love** should NEVER be rushed. Only time will tell if this is the person you are meant to spend your life with. Love is patient. Be like love.

Some of the very best romantic relationships first started out as a friendship. When the threat of a breakup comes to a solid relationship, the thought of losing your friend overrides the threat of losing a boyfriend only. You realize the value of your friend and then do what's necessary to repair the relationship because of the friendship.

*If you fail to set* **boundaries** *for yourself, other's will be "forced" to do it for you.*

That Ain't Love

# SETTING NON-NEGOTIABLE STANDARDS

*Maria was raised by her mother and grandparents in Louisville, Kentucky. Her grandfather often spoke with her about making good choices throughout her lifetime. He assured her that if she made good choices, she would achieve good success. He taught her the value of hard work and dedication. These lessons showed anytime Maria ran on the track.*

*As a freshman, a few weeks after her first tryout, Maria finished third at her first meet. In the coming seasons, she became a four-time winner at the meet. Her senior year, Maria finished second in the 400m at the Indoor Track & Field Championship. Maria was destined for Olympic greatness until her life took an unfortunate turn. The summer before her freshman year of college, Maria connected with fellow teammate Rita Woods. They hit it off almost instantly.*

*Unlike Maria, Rita was an athlete by force not by choice. Her father was a wrestling coach and her mother played tennis and ran track in college. Rita's cool, care free, bad-girl image impressed Maria. Rita introduced Maria to a different crowd of people than she was used to being around. Maria connected with one of the younger guys in the group named Angelo. Rita and Angelo convinced Maria to help them rob an elderly couple in Rita's neighborhood. Maria was told that all she had to do was keep an eye out. At first Maria was totally against it but after they promised that no one would be harmed, she agreed. During the robbery shots were fired. The teens fled the scene, leaving the elderly woman's husband lying in a pool of blood. The three were later caught and convicted. At nineteen years old, Maria was given fifteen years in prison.*

The word standards is defined as: morals, ethics, habits, established by authority, custom, or an individual as acceptable

Ask yourself the following questions:

1. *Do I have self-control?*
2. *Do I value myself?*
3. *Am I easily influenced?*
4. *Do I trust myself completely?*
5. *Do I make good choices?*
6. *Am I trust worthy?*
7. *Do I compromise my standards?*

Self-evaluation is essential. Asking yourself these kinds of questions will let you know if you have set healthy boundaries for your life. In order to have a healthy relationship you must first set non-negotiable standards. Non-negotiable standards not only keep you from living and loving beneath your standards but they will remind you of your ultimate goals. Goals are reminders of what YOU want to accomplish. Setting goals along with non-negotiable standards will guarantee you success in every area of your life.

COMPROMISING YOUR STANDARDS WILL SABOTAGE YOUR DESTINY...

Compromise is healthy when two mature people use it to make a mutual agreement. When used properly both parties walk away feeling like a winner. Unhealthy people can't understand compromise. They only imagine "winner take all" scenarios, leaving their partner utterly defeated.

Unhealthy compromise is sometimes used by individuals to satisfy their own immediate needs or desires. It is also often used when a person suffers from insecurity issues. They compromise their standards because they feel they can't do better. One may compromise their standards as it relates to a mate, a job or even friendship. In the end, the person who does the compromising is left feeling empty and unsatisfied.

Compromise is like starvation. The hunger pains make you feel as if you NEED something, anything, at that very moment. In desperation you eat whatever is available. The hunger temporarily disappears and you are content until the emptiness returns. Suddenly, you regret eating the first thing available and you wish you had pressed through the pain and waited for something much better for you.

**How to Set Realistic, Non-negotiable Standards**

1. Remind yourself of your non-negotiable standards often. This will help you when meeting people or when you are put in situations that challenge your beliefs.

2. Discuss your non-negotiable standards with others. No one can read your mind. If people aren't aware of your standards, then they can't abide by them. Set the record straight from day one.

3. Abide by your standards. Set the standard, people will only do what you allow them to do.

4. Believe in yourself and the standards that you have set for your life, no matter who disagrees do not allow anyone to devalue your standards.

Setting non-negotiable standards does not guarantee that you will never experience heartbreak. It will however, protect you from less of them.

*Wonder woman should not be the greatest female **SUPERHERO** of all time!*

That Ain't Love

## YOU HAVE THE POWER

*Kym loves men that aren't available. She knew at an early age that she was different than most girls; she wanted the guys that were involved. Something about the chase of a man who is involved turns her on. Kym's fetish has presented a lot of problems. One night after being cornered by a man's girlfriend and three of her friends, Kym was beaten unconscious. She's been in several altercations with women, chased from homes, cursed out, jumped, bullied and even stabbed. Kym has lost several friends and made double the amount of enemies. With all that she has suffered, Kym continues to love men that can't love her back. Kym has officially lost her power.*

---

**Do we know the power we possess?**

If women everywhere knew how much power they really possessed, maybe compromise would be less attractive in hopes of snagging a good mate. If we knew that we were designed with a powerful purpose in mind, would it change how we viewed ourselves?

A friend told me that a guy asked to take her sister out to a fancy restaurant. At the end of the delicious and expensive meal, she was told, "You need to pay for your own meal." My sister's friend was fine with doing that. What took the cake however, was when he "jokingly" asked her to come over to his house for a nightcap. I'm sure the look on her face, "Fool please," was the hint he needed to leave quickly and never call her again.

<u>So many questions . . . So little time</u>

- *Why did he feel comfortable asking a woman he hardly knew, to come to his apartment?*
- *Does the thought of possibly "getting some" erase the concern that something bad could happen to him?*
- *What type of women is he used to dealing with?*
- *Would another woman have gone to his apartment?*
- *Has this worked on other women?*

During a relationships presentation, I often give my male students a scenario. I ask them, "If you pay for prom, what does your date owe you in return?" Some said "a thank you would be nice" but majority say, "I better be getting some butt that night."

**Sex is often expected...**

- *Why is sex looked at as payment for "good deeds" sown?*
- *Why is sex automatically expected?*
- *Who came up with this crap?*

Why would someone suggest sex, as a way to show gratitude for something done or given? Every time a woman gives in to these types of stereotypes, she gives away not only her **power**, but also another woman's **power**. In some cases, I believe that good men are hard to find because of women that don't know their worth, make it hard for women that do.

**Scenario A:**

*If the person you are dating expects sex and you have sex with him solely based on his expectation, then you've given away your power. The next woman that this same person dates will then be expected to do the same.*

**Scenario B:**

*So the person you're dating expects sex from you. You let him know that you're not willing to have sex. He goes to another woman and she says, "no." He goes to another woman and she says, "no." More than likely he will go back to the first woman that respected her values and refused to lower her standard and respect her rules. That, is using your POWER.*

You set the standard in your dating relationships. A person will only do what you allow. When you fail to make boundaries and stand by them, you give away your power. Power and control are two very different things. You cannot control others but you can control you. Self-control is a SUPER POWER no villain can ever defeat. Try using your super power and see if your life changes for the better.

That Ain't Love

*If you were appraised your value would be,*
***"PRICELESS!"*

That Ain't Love

# WORTH IT ALL

Sometimes you just need to hear…

**You** are valuable!
**You** are needed!
**You** are loved!
**You** are victorious!
**You** are brave!
**You** are inspiring!
**You** are remarkable!
**You** are beautiful!
**You** are important!
**You** are brilliant!
**You** are powerful!
**You** are victorious!
**YOU** are the vessel that God used to bring forth His son.
**YOU** are a life carrier.
**YOU** are a life giver.
**You are full of worth.**

**YOU** heal with your hugs and soothe with your touch.
**YOU** build with your words and guide with your wisdom.
**You are full of worth.**

**You Are A WOMAN…**
You are a woman…full of creativity!
You are a woman…full of grace!
You are a woman…full of endurance!
You are a woman…full of possibilities!
You are a woman…full of passion!
You are a woman…full of legacy!
**You Are A WOMAN!!!**


<u>I Am Not My Past</u>

I often wonder how many women feel devalued, unappreciated, overlooked and unloved. If your value is based on what others say, think, or feel about you then you're not alone. I too know the pain of living beneath my value. I have devalued my worth with pessimistic thinking and negative self-talk. I've threatened my destiny with fear of the future, insecurity and plain old pride. I've been misused, misunderstood and rejected but my past failures do not define my future's story. I am valuable!

Your past failures are not your future's story. You are valuable!

## WE ARE WOMEN

**We are WOMEN…**

We are fearfully and wonderfully made. We were carefully considered, well-crafted and perfectly designed.

**We are WOMEN…**

We are passion wrapped in flesh. Creativity coupled with sensitivity and formed from rib into CURVACEOUSNESS.

We are…

**W-O-M-E-N!**

We are…

**VALUABLE!**

We are…

**WORTH IT ALL!**

www.ingramcontent.com/pod-product-compliance
Lightning Source LLC
LaVergne TN
LVHW021355080426
835508LV00020B/2293